Utoya

Written by Edoardo Erba,
translated by Marco Young

T0382969

methuen | drama

LONDON • NEW YORK • OXFORD • NEW DELHI • SYDNEY

METHUEN DRAMA
Bloomsbury Publishing Plc
50 Bedford Square, London, WC1B 3DP, UK
1385 Broadway, New York, NY 10018, USA
29 Earlsfort Terrace, Dublin 2, Ireland

BLOOMSBURY, METHUEN DRAMA and the Methuen
Drama logo are trademarks of Bloomsbury Publishing Plc

First published in Great Britain 2024

Utoya © Edoardo Erba, 2015

Published by Arrangement with S&P Literary – Agenzia letteraria Sosia & Pistoia

Translation copyright © Marco Young, 2024

Edoardo Erba and Marco Young have asserted their rights under the Copyright,
Designs and Patents Act, 1988, to be identified as authors of this work.

Cover image: Mariano Gobbi

A catalogue record for this book is available from the British Library.

A catalog record for this book is available from the Library of Congress.

ISBN: PB: 978-1-3505-2851-2
ePDF: 978-1-3505-2852-9
eBook: 978-1-3505-2853-6

Series: Modern Plays

Typeset by Mark Heslington Ltd, Scarborough, North Yorkshire

To find out more about our authors and books visit
www.bloomsbury.com and sign up for our newsletters.

Riva Theatre and ZAVA Productions in association with Arcola Theatre presents

UTOYA

Written by Edoardo Erba

Translated by Marco Young

First performed at Arcola Theatre, London on 13 August 2024

INTERNATIONAL JOURNEY OF THE PLAY

The Italian version

Utoya was first staged in Prato in 2015, produced by Teatro Metastasio. It was directed by Serena Sinigaglia, with set design by Maria Pazzi. It was performed by Arianna Scommegna and Mattia Fabbris. After running for two seasons at Teatro Metastasio in Prato, the production toured to Festival dei due Mondi in Spoleto and was recorded by RAI. Production rights were then acquired by ATIR in Milan, which produced the piece consecutively for another seven seasons. Utoya is currently still in the ATIR production catalogue. Marzorati for Milano Teatri: 'The dichotomies represented by the contrasts between the couples actually reside in the interiority of each of us [...] but the ultimate truth about our identity is denied us, or rather, is revealed precisely through fragmentation.'

The German version

Utoya received its German-language premiere at the Oldenburg Staatstheater in August 2017, translated by Sabine Heymann and directed by Peter Hailer. It was performed by Janine Kreß, Matthias Kleinert, Helen Wendt, Thomas Birklein, Franziska Werner and Fabian Kulp. After Oldenburg, the German production of *Utoya* was also performed at the Neue Bühne in Senftenberg. Michael Laages (Die Deutsche Bühne): 'the central horror of the Norwegians becomes clearly recognisable in the work of the Italian Erba: that it was one of us who turned into a monster, one like everyone else, only a little different'.

The Greek version

Utoya was produced by KMTD Productions at the Argo Theatre in Athens from 31 January to 31 March 2024. It was performed by Elena Moundovalis and Thodoris Gogos, and directed by Thodoris Gagos, with translation by Elena Moubndouvalis and musical supervision by Vassilis Kontaxis. Magda Basiou, for OpenMind theatre music books: 'a shocking, topical show that delicately touches on many issues plaguing contemporary society'.

WRITER'S NOTE

I wrote *Utoya* ten years ago, in a very different political context to that of 2024. The appalling terrorist act, which cost the lives of sixty-nine young socialists, seemed an isolated incident, in a Europe that appeared to possess adequate antibodies to counteract the criminal right. Today, however, a widespread disaffection towards politics has alienated the majority of Europeans from exercising a fundamental democratic right, the right to vote. And extreme right-wing movements, exploiting a fear of globalisation, immigration, technological innovation, and climate change concerns, have gained support, resurrecting the spectre of the terrorising years of Nazism and fascism. In the United States, too, where the leader of a coup threatens to become President, right-wing violence frightens those who cherish the rule of law, the division of powers, the freedom of expression. In a word, democracy. In this international context, it seems to me that my text is more relevant than ever.

My reflection in *Utoya* focuses on three themes: the value of political faith, obedience to orders and privacy. Each of these three elements is represented by a pair of characters. None of the three couples are directly affected by the attack, but all three are very close to the event, as if on the edge of a black hole. The choice of this audience position allows us to participate in the characters' emotions, but also in their reflections, which occur simultaneously and characterise every line of the play. The result is a tense, vibrant drama, filmically engaging, but retaining the reflective space that every good play must have.

I owe this piece to the encouragement of a great Italian director, Serena Sinigaglia, who pushed me to write about a difficult subject for a writer of comedies like me. And to Luca Mariani, author of *The Silence about the Lambs* – a precise documentation of the Norwegian massacre – who was the play's historical and scientific consultant. I feel this piece in some way belongs to them, too, and I thank them for their generosity in helping me.

Edoardo Erba

DIRECTOR'S NOTE

Utoya is not an easy play to sit with. It stays firmly on the sidelines of one of the most horrifying attacks of recent history and takes a clear sighted, albeit discomfiting look, at how those on the peripheries react to such violence. One of the most confronting provocations it offers to an audience is that tragedy can divide as often as it unites.

I have found myself returning to the concept of division throughout my work on the play, in which we see divides play out across political, gendered and deeply personal lines. Each couple stands on either side of a line in the sand, seemingly unable to reach across. The inability of these characters to communicate, to find common ground, is echoed by a society that finds itself ever more siloed. That this remains as true in the UK today as it was in Italy in 2015 (when the play was first staged) or Norway in 2011 is telling.

Edoardo Erba looks at his characters with an eye that is neither wholly sympathetic, nor wholly damning. Instead, we see people responding in the best way they know how to truly horrific circumstances. Crucially, these responses lay bare the characters' value systems in a way that invites an audience to examine their own. Most troubling among the beliefs unearthed are the assumptions around 'us' and 'them' and the no-longer-latent Islamophobia in their initial reactions. These assumptions are, of course, shattered but no narrative is offered to take their place. What is revealed is uncomfortable, and it is meant to be so. If Erba does not offer us a resolution or clear way forward within the pages of this play, it is because one has not yet been found. What the play does offer its audience is a warning and a provocation. A warning that this radicalisation, this far-right insurgence with its tendency towards violence, can happen here, now, to 'one of us'. And a provocation to look at the deepening divides in our society while we can still do something to breach them.

Sarah Stacey

TRANSLATOR'S NOTE

I came across *Utoya* in 2020 and was drawn in by the intelligent, sensitive way Edoardo had considered a deeply tragic event. *Utoya* places us at one remove from the tragedy, enabling us to feel the pain of the characters without sensationalising or platforming the extremism that caused it. Rather, it's much more about human behaviour in moments of crisis, and we're a fly on the wall as these individuals both succeed and fail to connect with one another in an increasingly chaotic situation. This piece invites us to reflect on how tragedy can pull people together but also drive them further apart, and how hate and extremism writ large can be fostered when, throughout society on a domestic level, we don't listen to people with differing views or attitudes from us, and people we deem 'other'. In 2024, as far-right populism still continues to enact influence across the globe, *Utoya* is as pertinent as ever, encouraging its audience to both eschew extremism and facile answers to society's problems, and reflect on how we might best treat those around us with empathy and compassion.

Tonally, this piece has been a wonderful challenge. Alongside the delicate portrayal of communication in crisis, I was surprised by the humour and warm affection sensitively woven throughout the script, counterbalancing the high stakes of the situation. As a translator, it is always so exciting to work on texts which have this mix of registers and styles within them, and it's been a pleasure to try my best to render them in English.

Marco Young

Supported by: Sue Whitley OBE, Guy Stobart, Sue Heathcote and Bill Heathcote, WellTax, Keith Sykes, Anglo-Norse Society, Maria Björnson Memorial Fund, Com.It.Es di Londra, Italian Cultural Institute, Unity Theatre Trust and Cambridge Online Tutors.

CAST

MALIN, UNNI, INGA | KATE REID

GUNNAR, ALF, PETTER | MARCO YOUNG

Kate Reid | Malin, Unni, Inga

Kate is a Northern Irish-English writer-performer who trained at Bristol Old Vic Theatre School (2016–2018). Theatre credits include: *The 4th Country* (Park Theatre); *A Girl, Standing* (Theatre503); *Refract* (King's Head Theatre); *January* (White Bear Theatre); *Lemons, Lemons, Lemons, Lemons, Lemons* (Wardrobe Theatre); *Measure for Measure* (Cambridge Arts Theatre). Workshops include: *Touching The Void* (Bristol Old Vic); *BOD* (Young Vic); *The Cleaner* (Traverse Theatre). Screen credits include: *The Other Half* for Ranga Bee Productions (Dave Channel); *Screening* for Airlock Films. She was a finalist for both Pleasance Theatre's Charlie Hartill Award (2020) and Sister and South of the River Productions' Screenshot Award for writer-performers at the Royal Court (2021). She is represented by Laura Stokes at The Artists Partnership. www.katereid.co.uk

Marco Young | Gunnar, Alf, Petter

Marco trained at Bristol Old Vic Theatre School. Stage credits include: *Sorry We Didn't Die at Sea, Another America* (Park Theatre); *The Life and Adventures of Santa Claus* (Pitlochry Festival Theatre); *My Cousin Rachel* (Bath Theatre Royal and UK tour); *The Stranger on the Bridge* (Salisbury Playhouse/Tobacco Factory and SW tour); *Macbeth*, *Romeo and Juliet* (Guildford Shakespeare Company); *A Girl, Standing*, (Theatre503); *Me and My Left Ball* (Tristan Bates); *Measure for Measure*, *Henry V* (Cambridge Arts Theatre). Workshops: *Lasagne* (King's Head); *HighTide Rising* (HighTide Theatre). TV includes: *Big Boys* S2 (Channel 4/Roughcut). Video game: *Company of Heroes 3* (Relic Entertainment).

CREATIVE TEAM

WRITER | EDOARDO ERBA

DIRECTOR | SARAH STACEY

TRANSLATOR | MARCO YOUNG

SET AND COSTUME DESIGNER | CAITLIN MAWHINNEY

LIGHTING DESIGNER | CATJA HAMILTON

SOUND DESIGNER | JAMIE LU

NORWEGIAN CULTURAL CONSULTANT | RUNA RØSTAD AUGDAL

PRODUCTION STAGE MANAGER | FAE HOCHGEMUTH

MARKETING MANAGER and CONTENT CREATOR | MEGAN GIBBONS

ARTWORK, PHOTO and VIDEOGRAPHER | MARIANO GOBBI

RIVA THEATRE | PRODUCER

ZAVA PRODUCTIONS | CO-PRODUCER and GENERAL MANAGER

Edoardo Erba | Writer

Edoardo is an Italian playwright, screenwriter, novelist, stage director and university professor (Pavia University, National Academy Silvio D'Amico and Belle Arti University of Rome).

The plays he's written include: *Porco Selvatico* (1991); *The Night of Picasso* (1991); *Blinde Curve* (1992); *Marathon* (1993); *The Family Vice* (1993); *Smallpox* (1998); *The Man of my Life* (1999); *The Salesmen* (1999); *Déjà-vu* (1999); *Without Hitler* (2001); *The Builders* (2002); *Good News* (2002); *Animals in the Fog* (2005); *Italian Drama* (2006); *Margarita and the Cock* (2006); *Michelina* (2008); *The Trouts* (2009); *Travelling with Albert* (2010); *All the Best* (2011); *VeraVuz* (2014); *Italy 2010* (2014); *Utoya* (2015); *Nine* (2015); *The Mistress of the B&B* (2017); *Rosalyn* (2017); *Maurice IV* (2019); *The Invisible Husband* (2021); *The Honest Ghost* (2022).

His plays have been performed at Italian festivals (including Venice Biennale, Taormina Film Fest, Montepulciano and Todi Festival) and in Italy's most renowned theatres. Erba has won the most prestigious awards for Italian dramaturgy (Olimpici del Teatro, Riccione, Idi, Candoni and Salerno) and the Robinson Award for his first novel *Ami*. *Marathon*, his most famous and successful work, has been translated in seventeen languages. The script won the Candoni Award in 1992 and was then represented for the first time in Parma in 1993. After that, the play was staged in London (translation by Colin Teevan), Edinburgh, Wellington (NZ), Sydney, Boston (translation by Israel Horowitz), Barcelona, Buenos Aires, Rio De Janeiro, Zagreb, Sofia, Tel-Aviv, Mumbai, Hong Kong and Tokyo.

Sarah Stacey | Director

Sarah is a theatre director specialising in new writing. She trained on the Birkbeck Theatre Directing MFA (including residencies at Royal & Derngate and BOVTS) and was a 2023 JMK finalist.

Her directing work includes: the Fringe First winner *Beasts: Why Girls Shouldn't Fear The Dark* (Edinburgh Fringe, as co-director); *lenny.* (Theatre503); *If. Destroyed. Still. True.* (Hope Theatre) and *One Kiss* (Belgrade Theatre). She has also directed new writing at the Jermyn Street Theatre, Southwark Playhouse, The Bunker, The Arcola, Royal & Derngate and Theatre Royal Stratford East.

As an associate and assistant director her work includes: *A Midsummer Night's Dream* (RSC); *Unexpected Twist* (UK tour); *The Two Popes* (UK tour); and the Olivier-nominated *Our Lady of Kibeho* (Theatre Royal Stratford East).

She also works as a dramaturg on plays in development, and is a reader for the Papatango and Bruntwood prizes.

Marco Young | Translator

Marco is a British-Italian translator and actor. He trained at Bristol Old Vic Theatre School and the University of Cambridge. His translation of *Sorry We Didn't Die at Sea* by Emanuele Aldrovandi ran for a month Off West End at Park Theatre in September 2023 and was published by Salamander Street Press. An excerpt of his translation of Nalini Mootoosamy's *Bleach Me* will be published in *Asymptote Journal* (upcoming edition, autumn 2024). His translation of *Suburban Miracles* by Gabriele Di Luca was showcased at Camden People's Theatre in January 2023, and his translation of *Alarms!* by Emanuele Aldrovandi received a rehearsed reading at Omnibus Theatre in July 2023. He has translated texts by Stefano Massini and Davide Enia, and recently completed a commission for award winning playwright Fabio Pisano for a first English translation of his new play *Spezzata, Rapsodia (per intercessione del Silenzio)*. He was a mentee on the 2022–23 Foreign Affairs Theatre Translator Mentorship Programme, and a member of Mercury Theatre Colchester's Producer Development Programme 2022–23.

Caitlin Mawhinney | Set and Costume Designer

Caitlin was nominated for Best Designer at The Stage Debut Awards 2022 and awarded the Evening Standard Future Theatre Fund for Visual Design in 2021. She was recently a JMK finalist, creative associate at Jermyn Street Theatre, and a resident designer at New Diorama Broadgate. Hailing from Yorkshire, Caitlin works across the country and designs from her studio in East London.

Recent credits as designer include: *Everyday Non-sense* (Southbank Centre); *Pansexual Pregnant Piracy* (Soho Theatre); *No More Mr Nice Guy* (Nouveau Riche); *Camp Phoenix* (Zest Theatre); *Pop Music*, *Ladies Unleashed*, *Teechers Leavers 22'* (Hull Truck Theatre); *The Cyclops*, *The Island of the Sun* (National Theatre Public Acts); *Dream School* (The Space); *Acid's Reign* (VAULT Festival); *The Anarchist* (Jermyn Street Theatre); *My Voice Was Heard But It Was Ignored* (Red Ladder Theatre Company/UK tour).

Catja Hamilton | Lighting Designer

Catja is a freelance lighting designer and co-director of Airlock Theatre. She is a former creative associate at Jermyn Street Theatre and resident designer at NDT Broadgate. Her previous credits include: *Talawa Firsts on Tour* (Talawa Theatre); *Pansexual Pregnant Piracy*, *Lesbian Space Crime* (Soho Theatre); *Scarlet Sunday* (Omnibus Theatre); *The Pursuit of Joy*, *The Anarchist*, *The Oyster Problem* (Jermyn Street Theatre); *The Wolf, The Duck, and The Mouse* (Unicorn Theatre); *Passing*, *Another America*, *The 4th Country* (Park Theatre); *Rip Van Winkle* (Hoxton Hall); *The Importance of Being... Earnest?* (UK tour); *Sorry We Didn't Die at Sea* (Park Theatre); *Birthright* (Finborough Theatre); *Agrippina* (Jackson's Lane); *Snail*, *Acid's Reign* (VAULT Festival); *Cassandra* (UK tour); *Time and Tide* (UK tour); *Paradise Lost* (The Shipwright); *An Intervention* (Riverside Studios); *Lizard King* (UK tour).
www.catjahamilton.github.io

Jamie Lu | Sound Designer

Previous work at the Arcola includes: *Spin* (2024); *Gentlemen* (2023); *The Apology* (2022); *We Started to Sing* (2022) and *Broken Lad* (2021). Theatre credits as sound designer include: *I'm Gonna Marry You Toby Maguire*, *Smoke*, *Tokyo Rose* (Southwark Playhouse); *George*, *Tiger* (Omnibus Theatre); *The Haunting* (New Vic Theatre); *The Government Inspector* (Marylebone Theatre); *English Kings Killing Foreigners*, *Mother's Day*, *Grills*, *Declan* (Camden People's Theatre); *Ada* (National Youth Theatre); *Transit* (The Space); *Shakespeare's R&J*, *Hedda Gabler* (Reading Rep); *Sorry We Didn't Die at Sea* (Park Theatre/Seven Dials Playhouse); *1984* (London Youth Theatre); *Declan* (EdFringe23); *Spin* (Hope Theatre/EdFringe23); *Going For Gold*, *Road* (Chelsea Theatre); *Burnout* (R&D, VAULT Festival and tour); *Still Here* (Jack Studio Theatre); *Iphigenia* (Hope Theatre); *Fester* (Bridge House Theatre); *A Gig for Ghosts* (Soho Theatre); *Paradise Lost* (Shipwright); *The Unicorn*, *What the Heart Wants*, *How to Build a Wax Figure* (Edinburgh Festival Fringe 2022); *The Blue House* (Blue Elephant Theatre); *Dirty Hearts* (Old Red Lion Theatre). As assistant sound designer: *Henry V* (Donmar Warehouse). Sound design for audio play: *The Dream Machine* (Fizzy Sherbet). www.jamieludesign.com

Runa Røstad Augdal | Norwegian Cultural Consultant

Runa is a director, writer and actor and has recently achieved her MFA in Theatre Directing from East15 Acting School. Originally from Trondheim, Norway, Runa received her bachelor's degree in drama and theatre from the Norwegian University of Science and Technology where she received an internship with the Giraffe Theatre Company which advocates and focuses on teens and adults with disabilities through inclusive theatre practices and performances. She was assistant director of *Bard in the Yard*, which was performed all over the UK to great public and critical acclaim (*The Guardian*, *The Telegraph*, *The Independent*). Before being accepted in the East 15 MFA Theatre Directing program, Runa established a theatre company Dragvollrevyen, with fellow colleagues, and directed their first show *Kaste stein I glasshus* which was nominated to participate in the semi-finals of the Norwegian Championship of Satire Theatre (NM I Revy).

Riva Theatre | Producer

Riva Theatre is a new London-based theatre company co-founded by Marco Young and Daniel Emery, focused on bringing plays from abroad to UK stages. Riva's first production, of award winning Italian play *Sorry We Didn't Die at Sea,* by Emanuele Aldrovandi, ran at Park Theatre in September 2023 to critical acclaim, following a first staging at Seven Dials Playhouse in July 2022. It was the first contemporary Italian play to receive a full Off West End run for over 20 years. Riva Theatre hosted a reading of Emanuele Aldrovandi's *Alarms!,* translated by Marco Young and directed by Daniel Emery, at Omnibus Theatre in 2023.

ZAVA Productions | Co-Producer and General Manager

ZAVA Productions is a UK theatre production company founded in 2022. They champion emerging writers and specialise in developing and producing original plays and musicals that reflect and question the society we live in. They are particularly interested in supporting inspiring works focusing on female voice and minority, ethnicity and gender discrimination, giving audiences the chance for a new awareness and perspective. They are dedicated to promoting Italian playwrights and composers to create a cultural exchange aiming to support and share stories that reflect universal experiences and enrich connections between Italian and international cultures. Productions include: *Hide and Seek* (VAULT Festival, February 2022 and Park Theatre, March 2023); *Utoya* (Arcola Theatre, August 2024), and *Miss I-Doll* (The Other Palace, spring 2025). www.zavaproductions.com

arcola
theatre

Arcola Theatre was founded by Mehmet Ergen and Leyla Nazli in September 2000. Originally located in a former textile factory on Arcola Street in Dalston, in January 2011 the theatre moved to its current location in a former paint-manufacturing workshop on Ashwin Street. In 2021, we opened an additional outdoor performance space just around the corner from the main building: Arcola Outside.

Arcola Theatre produces daring, high-quality theatre in the heart of East London. We commission and premiere exciting, original works alongside rare gems of world drama and bold new productions of classics. We work with creatives from across the globe, acting as a platform for emerging artists, providing them space to grow and explore, and similarly as a refuge for established artists refining their craft. Our socially engaged, international programme champions diversity, challenges the status quo, and stages trailblazing productions for everyone. Ticket prices are some of the most affordable in London, and we offer concessions for under 26s, senior citizens, those on disability benefits and unemployment benefits, as well as industry union members. We produce the yearly Grimeborn Opera Festival, hosting dozens of new and classical works from across the globe.

As part of our commitment to supporting the diversity of the theatre ecosystem, every year, we offer 26 weeks of free rehearsal space to culturally diverse and refugee artists; and our Participation department creates thousands of creative opportunities for the people of Hackney and beyond. Our pioneering environmental initiatives are award-winning and aim to make Arcola the world's first carbon-neutral theatre.

Arcola has won awards including the UK Theatre Award for Promotion of Diversity, The Stage Award for Sustainability and the Peter Brook Empty Space Award.

Artistic Director | Mehmet Ergen
Deputy Artistic Director & Executive Producer | Leyla Nazli
Marketing Manager | Millie Whittam
Marketing Assistant | Monique Walker

HVIS EN MANN KAN VISE SÅ MYE HAT.
TENK PÅ SÅ MYE KJÆRLIGHET VI KAN VISE SAMMEN.

IF ONE MAN CAN SHOW THIS MUCH HATE.
IMAGINE HOW MUCH LOVE ALL OF US CAN SHOW TOGETHER.

Stine Renate Håheim, survivor of Utøya

Utoya

Cast

Malin
Gunnar

Unni
Alf

Inga
Petter

The action takes place in Norway between 21 July and 21 August
2011.

The Night Before

1.

Gunnar *and* **Malin***'s flat in Bergen.*

Malin *is sitting on the sofa, reading an article.*

Malin   . . . And then we come to the striking Norwegian race, with their simple, proud beauty, their soft yet rugged looks. Generations of exposure to the Nordic climate have given them certain resilient traits. Their heads are triangular, with strong foreheads and sharp features. Their eyes are large, well-spaced from one another, and slightly oblique in shape. Norwegians are usually agile, muscular, and give off an aura of power and tranquillity. As far as personality goes, they are lively and alert, quickly forming attachments to particular people, who they then tend to follow everywhere. Though they are not antisocial or disinterested in others, they will be happiest sticking with their chosen person, both in downtime and in moments of stress or illness. Gunnar . . . are you listening?

No response.

Malin   Excellent hunters, Norwegians have exceptionally sharp nails and can catch birds in mid-air. They can also easily be kept on a short leash. If you ensure that your Norwegian Forest Cat always has something to play with and can exercise easily, you'll be rewarded with an extraordinarily faithful companion.

Gunnar *appears.*

His neck is tense, wearing glasses.

He is holding a closed book in his hand, a finger between the pages like a bookmark.

Gunnar   I don't want a cat in my house.

Malin   We could keep it in the guest room.

Gunnar   They drive you mad for years, then when they die
. . . it's really sad.

Malin   They're like people. They keep you company.

Gunnar   Animals should stay in the wild. The idea of
domesticating them is weird. Imagine a superior species
forcing us to pee in a box.

Malin   You sound like a Turk.

Gunnar   Why, what do Turks say about animals?

Malin   I don't know, but you don't see many dogs on leads
in Istanbul, do you?

Silence.

Gunnar   So?

Malin   What?

Gunnar   Continue the conversation. I was reading. You
called me through here. So continue.

Malin   I thought we were done.

Gunnar   No, you paused. You left that silence hanging
after Istanbul. As usual. When you want to talk about
something important, you go silent. What is it tonight?
What do you want?

Silence.

Gunnar   OK, fine, whatever . . . it's not like we have
anything particularly interesting to say anyway. Has Kristine
called from the camp?

Malin   No.

Gunnar   Good for her. She's having fun.

Malin *gives him an fiery look.*

Malin   I want a cat.

Gunnar   I want to read.

Malin   Norwegian, Siberian, Siamese . . . you decide the breed, but I want one.

Gunnar   Sometimes I feel like you do it on purpose. You think: what's the best way to irritate him? Make him lose his temper, turn it all into one big soap opera. One of those TV shows you sit and wallow over.

Malin   I'm going to get one tomorrow.

Gunnar   So the cat arrives and I leave? Is that the plan?

Malin *shrugs*.

Gunnar   I won't give you the satisfaction. If you get one, I'll hang it from the light fitting. A dead cat would be better than those God-awful crystal pendants your father gave us.

Malin   You're not funny.

Gunnar   I know, you've never liked my jokes. You think they're 'stupid and inappropriate'.

Malin   And yet you continue to make them.

Gunnar   I can't hide my light under a bushel! My mother always told me I was a funny kid. My grandmother too. I grew up believing in my humour. And my friends and teachers always found me hysterical at school. So you're late to the party – you can't hold me back.

Malin   You're so bitter.

Gunnar   *You're* the bitter one. And to get rid of it, you seek emotional tension. I just hate being interrupted when I'm reading.

Malin   We could all disappear for all you care, couldn't we? Me, Kristine, everyone. As long as you have your fucking books.

Gunnar   Yeah, basically.

Malin   I'm getting a cat, Gunnar.

Gunnar   Can we please stop this? If you love cats so much, buy a bunch of canned food, keep it in the garage, and go feed the strays in the park. Become a fully-fledged, crazy cat lady. You're reaching the right age and you dress like one anyway.

Malin   I'm going to get the cat from that shop on Strandgaten.

Gunnar   And I'm going to keep reading.

Gunnar *exits.* **Malin** *watches him leave. She is annoyed.*

2.

Honefoss Police Station.

Alf *is sat at a desk, in uniform.*

He's leafing through the sports section of a newspaper.

Unni *appears, also in uniform.*

She hands him a piece of paper.

Alf   What's this?

Unni   I'm taking my kids to their grandparents' in Kristiansund.

Alf   Are you from there? I didn't know that.

Unni   Bjarne is, not me.

Alf   Bjarne. So?

Unni   So I'd like to work a half-day tomorrow.

Alf   What's the issue?

Unni   I can make it up on Tuesday and work the night shift.

Alf   Great idea.

Unni   I'd leave at 14:00.

Alf   14:00.

He is about to sign the paper. He stops.

Unni   What's wrong?

Alf   Did you say tomorrow?

Unni   Yes.

Alf   Isn't it a bit late to file a request?

Unni   Bjarne and I decided at the last minute. We'd forgotten his mother's birthday.

Alf   This'll mess up the patrol rota.

Unni   I've already asked Nielsen. He can switch shifts.

Alf   Ah, you've already organised everything.

Unni   To make it easier for you.

Alf   Good.

Unni   Nielsen's all good for Friday.

Alf   Fine.

Alf *looks at her. As if waiting for something.*

Unni   Yes?

Alf   The thing is . . . it's up to me to organise it, isn't it? Not you.

Unni   I know, Alf. That's why I'm here asking you.

Alf (*thinks*)   No.

Unni   What? There's no reason to say no! Nielsen said . . .

Alf   I know what Nielsen said. And I don't give a shit.

Unni   Why do you always have to be so difficult?

Alf   I'm not being difficult. I'm saying no to a last-minute request.

Unni   It's no skin off your nose.

Alf   You want a Friday off? Great. You can have next Friday.

Unni   But I have to take my kids to their grandparents' tomorrow.

Alf   Well, I won't change a rota once it's been sent out.

Unni   Bjarne's away until Sunday, he's meeting us there. His mum's turning seventy, it's important . . .

Alf   To be honest, I couldn't care less about your domestic arrangements.

Unni   We promised her . . .

Alf   We have a patrol to carry out.

Unni   A patrol?

Alf   That student gathering, remember? On the island. Brundtland's going to give a speech there tomorrow.

Unni   So . . .?

Alf   So there has to be a police presence.

Unni   So what, Alf?

Alf   I'd rather be on patrol with you than Berg. He keeps farting in the patrol car.

Unni   Please. I'm asking you to do me a favour.

Alf   We'll have so little to do you'll be able to lie around and sunbathe.

Unni   You doing this on purpose?

Alf   Don't you like the view from there? It's romantic.

Unni   It is. Shame I have to go there with you though.

Alf   Maybe you got used to it with your friend Hagen. I don't have favourites.

Unni   Just tell me why.

They look at each other.

And don't give me this crap about a late request when two weeks ago you gave Jakobsen and Berg . . .

Alf *cuts her off.*

Alf   Shift's over. You'd better head home, or they'll be waiting for you tonight too.

Unni   My home is my business.

Alf   I was trying to be kind.

Unni   You're not able to be kind.

Unni *turns on the spot and exits.* **Alf** *turns back to the sports section.*

3.

Inga *and* **Petter**'*s farm in Asta.*

Inga *is staring out of the window.*

A tractor passes close by. **Inga** *shakes her head and sighs. A moment later* **Petter** *enters, boots and trousers all muddy.*

Petter   Is dinner ready?

Inga   Do you have any idea what time it is?

Petter   Is it ready or not?

Inga   I've already finished. I set the table. I cleared the table. I never know when you're going to show up. Whether you'll come back or not. Where have you been?

Petter   Weeding.

Inga   Don't give me that crap. The machinery's all still in the barn. You were out with the small tractor.

Petter   Oats are starting to ripen. It'll be a good harvest.

Inga   Answer my question.

Petter *laughs with embarrassment.*

Inga   Racing with that Kurd again.

Petter   Just to Glomma and back.

Inga   To *Glomma*?

Petter   And back.

Inga   Do you remember how much the tractor cost? We've still got two years of instalments to pay. And you're breaking it. You and that Kurd.

Petter   It's mine too. We're partners.

Inga   You're thirty years old, Petter. Not fifteen. I don't want to be looking after you like our mother. It's just the two of us now. It's up to us. And I'm tired. Do you get that? I'm tired.

Petter   It was just a bit of fun. After a long day at work.

Inga   What work? You haven't sorted the hay yet. It's been sitting there for fifteen days. Why haven't you done it yet? Do you want it to rot?

Petter   St Mary Magdalene's Day. Plenty of time.

Inga   What?

Petter   July 22nd. It's tomorrow.

Inga   Yeah, sure. Always putting it off until tomorrow.

Petter   Dad did it on Magdalene's Day.

Inga   Dad didn't let it rot. He used his brain. Clearly you've not taken after him.

Petter   I'm gonna make a Fenalar sandwich.

Inga   Let me do it, you'll cut it all wrong. Then you'll have to throw it away.

Inga *goes to prepare the sandwich.*

I don't want you becoming too friendly with the Kurd. He's our employee.

Petter   You said he's Norwegian like us.

Inga   Well, yes, but you still shouldn't be playing stupid games with him. Otherwise these people lose respect for us. They don't have our level of education.

Petter   D'you know his wife's pregnant? They're at it like rabbits. Nineteen years old, she's already got two.

Inga   Two kids, three kids, if they can manage it – who cares? What did Dad always say? Their house, their business.

Petter   No matter what way you turn, your arse is always behind you.

Inga   What?

Petter   Dad used to say that too.

Petter *laughs, grabs the sandwich and takes a bite enthusiastically.*

Inga   Have you fixed the netting out by the wood? Wolves'll get in. They'll wreck everything.

Petter   Yeah, yeah. I changed it this morning.

Inga   Praise the Lord. You actually did something.

Petter   I passed the troll on the way back.

Inga   Who?

Petter   Our neighbour. The guy who's rented the farm by the woods. I think he's a troll.

Inga   I don't care.

Petter   Why does he never say hello? He just stares. Never says anything.

Inga   I said I don't care.

Petter   D'you know what he was doing today? Loading a van.

Inga   So?

Petter   Well, I dunno. A new van. What's he loading?

Inga   That's his business.

Petter   I don't like him. He's got a weird face.

Inga   Well, it's not up to us, is it? Our face. Each person gets the face they get. Can't blame him for what he looks like.

Petter   He looks like he's made of rubber. It's gross.

Inga   You know, you should go and listen to the Reverend, rather than spending your Sundays drinking. Everyone's the same. Beautiful, ugly . . . respect everyone, as long as they don't bother you. Don't stick your nose into other people's business. Don't go snooping around their house. It's a form of respect. Good morning, good evening. That's it.

Petter   Right. Well, I said good morning, he didn't reply. Is there any beer?

Inga   You always look in the wrong place . . . it's back there.

Petter   Did you move it?

Inga   It's always been there. You always find it on the table because I put it there. Careful – you're dropping crumbs everywhere.

Petter *snorts.*

Inga *goes to get the bottle of beer.*

Petter *opens it with his teeth.*

He takes a swig.

Petter   I'm gonna watch a film.

Inga   I don't feel well. I'm going to bed.

Petter   Are you showering?

Inga   Maybe.

Inga *exits.*

Don't spy on me through the keyhole when I get undressed. You do realise I know you do that, Petter? I'll gouge your eye out with that screwdriver.

Unseen by her, **Petter** *shrugs his shoulders. Drinks.*

That Morning

4.

The farm. The television is still on. **Petter** *has fallen asleep in front of it, fully clothed.* **Inga** *enters in work clothes and sees him. She shakes him.*

Inga   Do you have any idea what time it is?

Petter   Why do you ask me the time whenever you see me?

Inga   Look at you. Not even making the effort to get to bed. And you stink. How much have you had to drink?

Petter   I dunno. It's hot. I was thirsty.

Inga   I've been out in the fields since seven. I'm knackered. I feel like I'm about to faint. You said you would sort out the hay.

Petter *finally gets up and goes to the window.*

Petter   Think it might rain. It's not the day for it.

Inga   Sure. You can't be bothered, that's your problem.

Petter *stretches.*

Petter   Look at those clouds. The ladleful of water for St Margaret's Day, right? That was two days ago. Could rain any moment now. Is there any coffee?

Inga   If you want coffee, get it yourself.

Petter   You should've married that factory guy who was after you.

Inga   The Moroccan? At my age? What are you on about?

Petter   Would've made you kinder, getting a bit of cock.

Inga   Watch your mouth. I'm your sister. I hate it when you're so rude.

Petter   You should've married him.

Inga   Well why don't you get married? Right age for it.

Petter   I'm happy being single.

Inga   Yeah, yeah, sure. Of course . . .

Inga *goes to the stove.* **Petter** *picks up a pair of binoculars and looks out of the window into the distance.*

Petter   You see that?

Inga   What?

Petter   He's not come back.

Inga   Who?

Petter   The troll. His van's not there. He parks it out front, but it's not there. He's stayed out all night.

Inga   Is that illegal?

Petter   And look how much fertiliser he's got in his yard . . . I was watching when they delivered the bags.

Inga   Why do you care?

Petter   He's not growing anything. Why does he need so much fertiliser?

Inga   Why don't we worry about not running out of ours? Did you order a new batch?

Petter   This afternoon. I'll do it this afternoon.

Inga   You're always putting things off! What use are you here? You've not studied, you don't do any work, you don't get anything done. How many times do I have to tell you; I'm tired and I don't feel well.

Petter   We don't need the fertilizer yet. Do you know who he is? Or where he comes from?

Inga   Who?

Petter   Our neighbour.

Inga   I'm not the registry office, am I? Put those bloody binoculars down.

Inga *grabs them from him.*

Petter *lingers a little longer by the window.*

Petter   What does he actually do?

Inga   Can't you read? (*Pointing at the neighbour's sign.*) Agricultural services.

Petter   But his fields are full of weeds.

Inga   So? There are plenty in ours too.

Petter   He doesn't have any tractors, any threshers . . .

Inga   I've put water on for the coffee. Hurry up. Go and wash or you'll never start the day.

Petter *leaves the window. He smells his armpits.*

Petter   I smell worse than the Kurd.

He exits. Then, from offstage:

He's always alone. Running a farm on his own?

Inga   No different here! Only difference is I'm a woman!

Inga *shakes her head. She goes to make* **Petter***'s coffee.*

5.

Gunnar *is having breakfast.*

He reads a newspaper while eating.

Gunnar   Where did you get this salmon?

No answer.

Gunnar *raises his voice a little.*

Where did you get this, Malin?

Malin *responds from offstage.*

Malin   At the market.

Gunnar   It's poorly smoked.

Malin   There's cheese too.

Gunnar (*speaking to himself about the rest of his plate*)
Cucumber and beans. Great.

Malin *enters.*

Malin   I spoke to Kristine.

Gunnar   When?

Malin   Just now.

Gunnar   They're getting her up nice and early. Good. She
never emerges before noon at home. What did she say?

Malin   Nothing.

Gunnar   What do you mean, nothing? How's she doing,
what's she up to?

Malin   She asked if we could load some money onto the
prepaid card.

Gunnar   Wasn't the camp all-inclusive?

Malin   I told her I'd put a thousand krone on it.

Gunnar   Well make it your money then, because I don't
agree with that. She's spoilt. She does nothing all day. She
only opens her mouth to ask for money.

Malin   She's not even sixteen years old.

Gunnar   So?

Malin   She's still a child.

Gunnar   Exactly. Just wait until she's older. We'll have to re-mortgage the house every time she opens her mouth. What else did she say?

Malin   Nothing.

Gunnar   She only says things she shouldn't. She's taken after you.

Malin *drinks her coffee*.

Malin   I don't think she's having a good time.

Gunnar *shrugs*.

Malin   Why did you make her go?

Gunnar   I didn't want to watch her spend the whole summer lying on the sofa. Texting away on her phone.

Malin   Aren't we going to France in August?

Gunnar   Well, she'll just lie on the beach, won't she. Phone still in hand.

Malin   She's not enjoying herself, Gunnar.

Gunnar   Of course she is. There's lots of boys there, I'm sure she's having a good time.

Malin   I could tell from her tone.

Gunnar   How can you tell from her tone? She always sounds pissed off with us. She's rebelling. Right age for it. She should.

Malin   You know what'll happen when she's back? She'll hate us even more. This summer will be a nightmare.

Gunnar   We'll find some other place to send her to.

Malin   She won't go. She told us loud and clear – she let us have this one, but she's not going anywhere else.

Gunnar   Can we just stop worrying about her? The salmon was gross, now you're gonna make me throw the cucumber back up as well.

Malin   Bet she'll lose her virginity this weekend.

Gunnar   So she'll have had fun.

Malin   She'll do it just to spite us.

Gunnar   How do you know?

Malin   I know her.

Gunnar   Well, it was going to happen sooner or later. She's a bit behind compared to her friends anyway, isn't she? And if she's going to have sex, it might as well be with a socialist.

Malin   You're obsessed with these socialists.

Gunnar   Well, I *was one* when I was younger.

Malin   And now you're just a gross egotist.

Gunnar   Socialism is about bringing forward those who were born at a disadvantage. I can't remember who said that, but it's about people like you.

Malin   You turn everything I say against me.

Gunnar   So let's stop talking.

Malin   You shouldn't have forced her to go.

Gunnar   Can I finish my breakfast?

Malin   I didn't agree to it. I don't like socialists. I never have.

Gunnar   Oh you poor thing. Not your fault though, is it? Growing up surrounded by conservatives. Soaking up those right-wing thoughts since kindergarten. Seeing the state as a good disciplinarian parent. With an alcoholic grandfather and a tax evading father . . .

Malin   What's my dad got to do with anything?

Gunnar   Let me finish my food.

Malin   No, tell me.

Gunnar   Nothing. Your father never has anything to do with anything. He didn't see anything, didn't hear anything, didn't say anything. He wasn't there . . . the ghost man. More of a dense fog than a man. Sod the cucumber. I'm going to work.

Gunnar *gets up, leaving his food on his plate.*

Malin   Where are you going? We haven't finished talking.

Gunnar   I've got a class to teach.

Malin   There'll be a cat here when you get back. I've even chosen the name.

Gunnar   I've already warned you what I'll do to it.

Gunnar *exits.*

Malin *sits down to have her breakfast.*

Fuming.

6.

Alf, *at the Police Station.*

He is waiting for **Unni**, *who is changing into her uniform.*

Alf   We're late.

Unni *doesn't reply.*

Alf   The car's out front. You're driving.

Unni *continues to get dressed.*

Alf   My wife made sandwiches. There's one for you too if you want, she always makes too many. We'll just get something at the services tonight.

Alf *tries to catch a glimpse of* **Unni** *dressing.*

Alf She's always worried I'll go hungry. If I do get hungry, the last thing I want are her sandwiches. Do you know how many there are?

Unni How many sandwiches?

Alf Students.

Unni I have no idea.

Alf I reckon five or six hundred, but I'm not sure. Three days in the middle of the woods at the party's expense. No sex allowed. Officially. No beer allowed either, but I'm sure they'll have litres of the stuff. They should be allowed to have fun. So when they get older they'll open up all our borders to the blacks. Ready?

Unni Not yet.

Alf Nielsen's worked the night shift, he'll lose it if we're any later. How did you leave things with the in-laws?

Unni Why do you care?

Alf Just asking.

Unni *comes out in uniform.*

Alf *looks at her intently.*

Alf You look good in uniform. I'd never noticed.

Unni Continue to not notice.

Alf Oh come on, we've got to spend the whole day together. Let's try and have a laugh and not get off on the wrong foot.

Unni Well, given how you treated me yesterday . . .

Alf I know, I get it. But you women always know how to get men to treat you better. Just saying, for next time. But you already know that full well, don't you, Unni.

Unni What are you saying?

Alf   I manage the patrol rota, don't I. I managed it even when I wasn't in charge.

Unni   So what?

Alf   You and Hagen did a fair few patrols together, didn't you? Before he was sent off to Command.

Unni *stares at him.*

Alf   But I didn't say anything. None of my business, is it? Lips sealed.

Unni   Listen to me, Alf. I don't know what you're trying to get out of this patrol . . .

Alf   What are you on about?

Unni   But if you drop one more perverted hint like that again, I'll report you for harassment.

Alf *laughs.*

Alf   Harassment . . .

Unni   I hate men like you. How you half-say things, just implying, just giving us the gist. I think you're all fucking creeps. Absolutely not. You want some of this? Fucking pay me. You think you can do whatever you like, whenever you want? Not with me. I've got enough going on already.

Alf   Like what? Granny's birthday?

Unni *gives him a hateful stare.*

Alf   Skipping your mother-in-law's knees up didn't go down well, did it? I get it. It's peak salmon season, isn't it – mid June, lower water levels. Does your husband fish?

Unni   No.

Alf   I see. Well, he's fished a sour one for a wife, hasn't he?

Unni   Fuck you.

Alf   As your elder and your superior, I'll pretend I didn't hear that.

Alf *heads off.*

Unni *stays where she is.*

She hesitates. Considers bailing.

She then follows him.

The First Attack

7.

The countryside.

Unni *rushes in, out of breath.*

Unni   Alf? Where are you, Alf?

Alf *replies from offstage.*

Alf   What took you so long? I told you to move the car into the shade, not take a nap on top of it.

Unni   There's been an explosion at the Parliament Building.

Alf   What?

Unni   I just heard it over the radio. They're saying people have died. Alf!

Alf *enters, doing up his fly.*

Alf   Where? Here in Norway?

Unni   At the Parliament Building, our government.

Alf   Can't be true.

Unni   It's definitely true. It happened. It literally just happened.

Alf   You must have misheard.

Unni   I'm not an idiot, Alf. They said it blew out all the windows within a 500 metre radius.

Alf   Who's they?

Unni   I just called Command at Oslo. Olsen or Jensen, I'm not sure who it was. All the patrols are heading there now.

Silence.

Alf   How many dead?

Unni   They don't know.

Alf   Did the building collapse?

Unni   No. I don't think so. Maybe some of it. I don't know.

Alf   When did it happen?

Unni   Just now. Five minutes ago.

Alf   Fuck.

Alf *takes out his mobile and makes a call.*

Alf   Why are they not picking up . . .

Unni   I tried too, nothing.

Alf   Give us some orders, at least! Fuck!

Unni   We should grab the car and get over there. They'll need us.

Alf *dials another number.*

Alf   Not without orders. Pick up, Arild, come on . . .

Unni   They're all be on patrol.

Alf   Exactly, they should pick up. (*His call is answered.*) Arild . . . oh, fucking hell, why didn't you pick up sooner? Can you tell us . . . ah . . . OK . . . yes, but what else? We can head over there too if you need us . . . I understand that, but there's nothing for us to do here so we might as well . . . he hung up.

Unni   What did he say?

Alf   A van full of explosives. There's a body hanging from one of the windows.

Unni   What about the ministers?

Alf   They think they're all fine, none of them were there. That lot always cover their own arses.

Silence.

Unni We should arm.

Alf Why?

Unni It's an emergency. We're under attack.

Alf What attack? Do you see any attack here? What do you want to do, shoot at the birds? There's a procedure for taking up firearms, we need authorisation. You should know that.

Unni Just as well I sent the kids to Kristiansund. Thank God for grandparents. I'd be losing it if they were in town. I'd go get them straight away.

Alf You'd go if I gave you permission. We're the police, not the boy scouts.

Unni Alf, please. Look, I'm sorry I got annoyed about the rota, but we've got to work together now.

Alf Weren't you going to report me for harassment?

Unni They've attacked the Government Building. For all we know, they could be after the King next.

Alf Go on, move that arse and go get the car.

Unni *turns to go.*

Alf *slaps her on the backside.*

Unni *turns around.*

Alf *looks at her mockingly.*

Alf No tan today.

He looks at his watch.

Brundtland must be on the island by now. Back to the office.

Unni *doesn't react.*

She moves away.

Alf *watches her.*

He spits on the ground.

8.

The farm in Asta.

Inga *is chopping fruit.*

The phone rings.

She goes to answer the call.

Inga   Hello?

Petter *is at a bar.*

Petter   Have you seen what's happened?

Inga   Where?

Petter   In Oslo. A bombing.

Inga   How do you know?

Petter   Turn the TV on, you'll see it.

Inga   Aren't you out on the tractor?

Petter   I'm in town. At a bar. I came in to buy cigarettes.

Inga   Is this how you work? You haven't tidied anything out there, and now you're in town . . .

Petter   Inga, they've attacked the Government Quarter.

Inga   Who has?

Petter   I don't know. Terrorists. Muslims. Them.

Inga   *Here?* Petter have you been drinking again?

Petter   Turn on the TV if you don't believe me.

Inga   There aren't any terrorists here.

Petter   Well, looks like they've arrived.

Inga   I don't believe you.

Petter   Turn on the TV.

Inga   It must be a film.

Petter   There's been an attack. They've just announced it.

Inga   Don't shout, everyone will hear you.

Petter   Everyone here knows what's happening. *Boom*, at the Parliament Building. An explosion.

Inga   I don't believe you, OK? I don't believe you because that sort of stuff doesn't happen here. You're trying to frighten me. Another one of your stupid jokes. I'm not falling for it.

Petter   Turn on the fucking TV!

Inga *hesitantly leaves the conversation and goes to turn the TV on. She sees the early footage of the attack.*

Petter   So? See it now?

Inga *freezes for a moment, astonished.*

Inga   Yeah, I see it, but that can't be here. That's not Oslo. I know Oslo. I've been there. It's not Oslo.

Petter   It's Oslo.

Inga   It must be . . . Baghdad. They're always showing things from over there. That's Baghdad, not Oslo.

Petter   Look at the headline at the bottom. Oslo.

Inga   Yeah, it says Oslo but it's not. It's a mistake. That's not Norway. That's not our country.

Petter   Everyone here's talking about it. They're all terrified.

Inga   They're talking about it but it's not true.

Petter   See their faces? See the policemen? They're blond. It's us, Inga. They've attacked us.

Inga   I don't believe you.

Inga *looks up and looks out of the window for a moment. Suddenly, she puts the phone down and moves towards the window.*

Petter   If I see those guys I'll break their necks. You hear me, Inga? Don't tell me they're Norwegians like us. I'll break their necks.

No response.

Petter *stands up for a moment, holding the phone. He is agitated and frightened.*

He hangs up.

9.

Malin *is watching television.*

We hear the audio of the attack with no commentary.

Gunnar *enters.*

Gunnar   Did you see?

Malin   Insane.

Gunnar   They're saying people have died.

Malin   I've been crying. God. Can you believe it?

Gunnar   Have they said who did it?

Malin   They reckon it could be an Islamist cell.

Gunnar   So the Prophet's started shitting on us here too.

Malin   Why are they targeting us? Why Norway?

Gunnar   Maybe they don't like the smoked salmon.

Gunnar *sits next to his wife to watch the television.*

Gunnar   What a fucking disaster. Tragedy.

Malin   I've always told you – life is better here in Bergen. Too many foreigners in Oslo. Far too much chaos.

Gunnar   What've foreigners got to do with anything? Don't start with your racist rants again. Please. I don't want to hear it in my house.

Malin   We're not safe, I've always said it. Too many dodgy-looking people around. I'm calling Kristine.

Gunnar   Why?

Malin   Because. I'm worried. I want to speak to her.

Gunnar   You'll just annoy her.

Malin   I want to hear my daughter's voice.

Gunnar   She's forty kilometres from Oslo. She's not in danger. I even gave her the phone number for the nearest police station. Leave her alone. She'll call if she needs us.

Malin *puts her phone down.*

Malin   Why do I always end up listening to you?

Gunnar   Because I'm always right.

Malin   I am so done with you.

She goes back to watching the footage on the television.

Malin   Bastards. We're a peaceful country. We don't step on anyone's toes.

Malin *suddenly has a thought.*

Malin   Isn't Dahl's office right on Mollergata?

Gunnar   Are Dahl? He's lived here for twenty years . . .

Malin   Oddmund Dahl. He used to do consultancy for MPs. Remember? We met him last winter in Turkey. The guy who danced tango.

Gunnar   I didn't like him.

Malin   You're so obnoxious. Who *do* you like? They were both lovely, him and his wife. She can't dance, though.

Malin *picks up her phone.*

Gunnar What are you doing?

Malin I'm calling them. I've got their number. I want to check they're OK.

Gunnar You don't even know them, why are you calling them at a time like this?

Malin I'm worried about them.

Gunnar We hung out with them for three days.

Malin We explored Cappadocia together. It was unforgettable.

Gunnar Why do you have to call anyone? I don't get it.

Malin *ignores him and makes the call.*

Malin Ingrid? Hi! It's Malin. Malin from Bergen, remember? Turkey, last winter . . . good thanks, I just wanted to check you were alright, I saw what happened in Oslo and . . . ah good. Good. What about Oddmund? Terrifying, I can imagine . . . ah, he's in France . . . good. No, it's just, they mentioned Mollergata, I immediately thought . . . ah, you're a bit further off . . . OK. I'm glad you're all OK . . . don't mention it . . . I just . . . what? A friend of yours? Well, it must be chaos . . . yes, I'll let you go, the phone must be ringing off the hook . . . I bet. Bye, Ingrid. Say hi to Oddmund.

Ends the call.

Malin Her husband is in France.

Gunnar We can all breathe a sigh of relief then.

Malin She says his office is about a kilometre further off. But a colleague of Oddmund's who was closer to the explosion says he saw an armed policeman driving the wrong way up the Mollergata.

Gunnar   Who cares? Can't be worrying about speed limits in a situation like that.

Malin   But our police don't carry firearms.

Gunnar   Even a blind dog finds a bone.

Malin   What?

Gunnar   Nothing. Thought it was the right moment for a proverb.

Malin   I wonder whether this guy told anyone? Do you think he did? Maybe we should call the police, just to be sure.

Malin *picks up her phone again.*

Gunnar   Are you insane? You're going to call the Bergen police to pass on something from a friend – who you don't even know – of a woman from Oslo you met at Christmas in Cappadocia?

Malin   It could be helpful.

Gunnar   Please can we stop making ridiculous phone calls. You're stressed, I get it, but we can't do anything about this. You want them to think you're insane? Don't waste their time with pointless calls. It's over. Enough now.

Malin   It's over?

Gunnar   Well, yes. Can't get any worse than this, can it? It's over. All they can do now is try to do right by the people who've died.

Malin   I've been stuck here for an hour. I can't focus on anything else.

Gunnar   At least you didn't go off and buy a cat.

Malin   Gunnar. Hug me.

Gunnar *exits.*

The television continues showing footage.

Malin *stays still, watching.*

The Island

10.

Honefoss Police Station.

Alf *is on the phone.*

Alf   Honefoss Police Station. What? . . . OK, can you start by giving me your name? Hello? I need your personal details – could you speak up, please? Gunshots? OK, stay calm and tell me who's shooting. I can't hear you . . . Where are you right now? What? Hello? Hello?

The line goes dead.

Alf *tries dialling the number again.*

No reply.

Unni *enters the scene.*

Unni   What's going on?

Alf   Fuck.

Unni   What's happening?

Alf   Where are Nielsen, Jakobsen and Berg?

Unni   Shopping for tonight.

Alf   All three of them? What the fuck, does it take three people to do the shopping? Call them immediately.

Unni   What's going on, Alf? Who was that?

Alf   I don't know. Didn't leave their name. They were on the island.

Unni   What island?

Alf   There's a gunman on the loose on Utoya.

Unni   What?

Alf   U-toy-a. It sounds like there's someone shooting at the student camp.

Alf *dials a number.*

Unni   The Labour Party youth camp?

Alf   Yeah.

Unni   Where's the island security?

Alf   I'm calling the guy now . . . He's not picking up. Fuck.

Unni   What the hell is happening, Alf? What is going on today?

Alf   How do I know? I know as little as you do.

Unni   Let's call Oslo.

Alf   Wait. The guy who called could just be a nutter, and not –

The office phone rings.

Unni *is the closest and picks up.*

Unni   Honefoss Police Stat – who is this? Who's speaking? OK, don't cry, calm down. Can you speak up . . . shooting? Yes, Yes . . . don't cry, stay calm . . . we'll be there . . . just say where . . . a policeman? Yes, we'll be there right away. What? I can't hear you, could you say that again? Where?

There is no reply.

Alf   Did they hang up?

Unni   It was a girl.

Alf   Did she say a policeman?

Unni   Yes. Heavily armed. She says he's slaughtering them like animals.

Alf   Where? What part of the island?

Unni   I don't know. She didn't manage to tell me. I could hear the gunshots. He must have been close.

Alf   Call her back and ask her. Come on, what are you waiting for?

Unni *calls back.*

There is no reply.

It's just ringing.

Alf   Fuck!

Unni   Do you think she's . . .

Alf   How do I know? Call the others.

Unni *calls them.* **Alf** *calls Oslo simultaneously. They talk over each other.*

Unni   Berg? It's Unni. What? No, no salmon, leave all of that and come back immediately . . . there's a situation on Utoya . . . at the camp, yes . . . no, leave everything and come back to the office. Now.

Alf   There's been an attack in Utoya . . . a guy in police uniform is shooting the kids at the camp . . . apparently . . . we're getting calls, they want our help . . . no, Bruntland has already left . . . we don't know . . . five, but only three of us are firearm-trained . . . OK, we'll await orders . . . I've put my men on standby.

Ends the call.

Unni   What did they say?

Alf   To stay calm.

Unni   Stay calm? Alf, let's go. Now.

Alf   No. We're got to await orders.

Unni   What orders?

Alf   From Oslo. They need time to monitor the situation and get organised. They'll be looking for a helicopter. They'll do a fly over of the island to see what's happening.

Unni   But we can't leave those kids alone.

Alf   We'll know what to do soon. They said they'd call back right away.

Unni   They can call our mobiles.

Alf   There's no service boat. How do we get to the island? Swim?

Unni   We can take one of the tourist boats. At the pier at Utvika.

Alf   We have to be authorised to use non-service vehicles. There's a whole procedure.

Unni   Who gives a shit, Alf? Those kids are being shot.

Alf   They'll enact countermeasures, don't worry.

Unni   Who? *We're* the police, Alf.

Alf   No, you're not the police. You're a single officer who counts for fuck all, undisciplined and emotional. You start crying and panicking as soon as there's an emergency, and calling me by my first name, as if we were related.

Unni   I can't believe this. You don't want to do anything? Someone is shooting those children and we're going to stay here to wait for orders? What, are you scared?

Alf   Get it together, Unni.

Unni   The girl on the phone must have been fourteen, fifteen at most. She was a child. She was crying. Maybe she was shot as she called me. What are we doing here? Don't you see this is fucking crazy?

Alf *doesn't respond.*

Unni   Make up your mind, or I'll go there by myself.

Alf *steps in front of her.*

Alf   You will not move an inch until I order you to. Sit down next to the phone. Run the comms. That's an order, Unni. Understood? An order. No discussion –

Unni *pushes* **Alf** *out of the way and exits.*

Alf *watches her angrily for a moment.*

He then follows.

11.

We hear the sound of the television.

Malin *is holding her phone.*

She is panicking.

Malin   She's not answering. Christ. She's not answering. Gunnar, it just keeps ringing.

Gunnar *replies from offstage.*

Gunnar   She must've left it somewhere.

Malin   I'm scared . . .

Gunnar *enters the scene, also clutching his phone.*

Malin   What're they saying?

Gunnar   Nothing. Just that there's been an attack . . . they say they can hear gunshots.

Malin   And they're not doing anything? Why are they not doing anything?

Gunnar   They will, they must just be getting organised.

Malin   Well, what are they waiting for, for him to kill all of them? Call the police! Call someone!

Gunnar   I just called them back and they said they're doing all they can.

Malin   All they fucking can! We've got to get her out. Do something, Gunnar!

Gunnar   Me? What can I . . .?

Malin   You're just standing there, dazed.

Gunnar   It's 450 kilometres from here to Utoya, with over 200 tunnels. Six hours by car. What am I supposed to do?

Malin   I will die, OK? I will literally die if I don't hear from Kristine.

Gunnar   Calm down. I left her name. They said they'll call when they know something.

Malin   Oh Christ, Christ . . . when they know something . . .

Malin *holds her head in her hands.*

Gunnar   Calm down.

Malin   Stop telling me to calm down. You're so annoying!

Gunnar   We have to wait. Have faith. Let's stay calm. That's all we can do.

Malin   I could *feel* something was wrong . . . why do I never listen to what I *feel*? That's always my problem, always just listening to what others think.

Gunnar   How could we have predicted something like this? Come on, you'll drive yourself mad. Sit down.

Malin   Can you at least shut up? Please?

Gunnar   So you're taking it out on me now?

Malin   Whose idea was it to send her to the camp?

Gunnar   Malin, please. I'm as stressed as you are, trust me. Now's not the time to get into all that.

Malin   I'm fed up of you deciding when we can talk about something, and when we can't. Drop the 'big shot professor' act. From now on, if I want to speak, I speak, understood?

Gunnar   OK, speak then. If you calm down, speak, Malin. Come on . . .

Malin *glances desperately at the phone.*

Malin   Why won't they call?

Gunnar   They'll call. Be patient. You'll see, it'll just be a couple of minutes. Come on, let's keep talking.

Silence.

Gunnar *sighs.*

The house phone rings.

Malin *dives to answer it.*

Malin   Hello? . . . Fuck! Fuck you and your fucking offers.

Malin *hangs back up.*

Gunnar *looks at her inquisitively.*

Malin   A phone company. Now is not the time. Fuck!

Gunnar   Well, how could they know . . .

Malin   Oh stop justifying everything!

Malin *looks anxiously at the television.*

Didn't you know that policeman? The father of that girl in third grade?

Gunnar   Yeah. They transferred him up north a few years ago.

Malin   Call him.

Gunnar   Why?

Malin   Call him, maybe he can do something.

Gunnar   What could he do, Malin? He's basically at the North Pole. What's he gonna do, toboggan all the way down?

Malin   Your daughter is there, Gunnar!

Gunnar   I know, stop reminding me!

Malin   So call him! Don't just sit there like an imbecile.

Gunnar   It's a national emergency. It's not just about us.
Try to stay rational. The whole of Norway is responding
to this.

Malin   Oh really? And why is that response not reaching
the island? Why are they leaving them alone? Fuck the
whole of Norway! My daughter is there.

Gunnar   I know, Malin. But they'll be there. They'll get
there soon.

Malin   'They'll get there soon.' Not the response I'd expect
from a father.

Gunnar   Look, sit down. Come on, be patient . . . I know
it's difficult. But we can't do anything about it. Sit here. Try
to think positivel –

Malin *turns and gives him a death stare.*

Malin   Shut up! You don't want to do anything? At least
shut up. Go through there. Fuck off!

Gunnar *lowers his gaze and exits.* **Malin** *continues panicking.*

12.

On the shore of Lake Tyri.

We can hear the echoes of gunshots.

Alf *looks into the distance.*

Unni *appears.*

The situation is very tense.

Unni   Listen to me, Alf.

Alf   No.

Unni   I said listen to me.

Alf *turns his back on* **Unni**.

Unni *grabs his shoulders and turns him back round.*

Unni   Do you hear that? Those are not fireworks. If I knew more about firearms, I could even tell you the calibre.

Alf *turns away again, as if to block out what she's saying.*

Unni   It's been over half an hour and still no call from Oslo. You have to listen to me.

Alf *still refuses to turn round.*

Unni   Alf, it's just the two of us here. No superiors. We'll say there was a request for immediate assistance, which there was. We'll say we couldn't reach them for authorisation. That the phone lines were down, which is possible. There are firearms in the car. Can we please not just stand here. The others are in the office fielding calls. We've got our mobiles, they can reach us immediately. Let's go, just the two of us. Come on, get the keys, open the boot and let's load the firearms onto one of those boats . . .

Alf   You're not even authorised to use them.

Unni   It's an emergency, do you get that? Rules don't count when it's an emergency.

Alf   Bullshit. An emergency is precisely when rules are required. How many terrorists are there?

Unni   They think there's only one.

Alf   We don't know that for sure. What are you basing that on? On phone calls from terrified kids? We don't know if there's only one. How are they attacking? What weapons do they have? We don't know.

Unni   So?

Alf   So, this is what the Special Forces are for. This isn't a job for us.

Unni   But the Special Forces are taking too long. Someone is attacking the kids *right now*. They're killing them one by one.

Alf   We don't know that.

Unni   Are you deaf? Can you not hear the gunshots?

Alf   Listen, I'm following the orders I received. And you will too, without saying a word. Is that clear?

Unni   You're hiding behind these orders, Alf.

Alf   Stop talking rubbish. We can't just do what we want. This is an organisation. A body. Do you get what that means? You and I are cells. There is a head which gives orders, at Oslo command centre. And if a cell rebels, it is no longer a cell, it's a cancer.

Unni   I don't give a fuck! Let's help these kids! I can't take it anymore, just standing here like a fucking lemon.

Alf   I am fucking done with your bullshit, OK? And not just today. Expect a report.

Unni   File all the reports you want. But *please* can we take that boat and *go*. Look, I'm asking you calmly. If you don't want to give me a firearm, I don't care, I'll go unarmed.

Alf   I will say this for the last time, Unni. We are not authorised to move from this location. End of discussion.

Unni   Why are you like this, Alf? Why don't you take responsibility in life? *Any* responsibility?

Alf   I obey my fucking orders! Without following orders, this uniform wouldn't exist. There would be no rule of law. No state.

Alf *starts shouting and* **Unni** *does the same.*

Unni   Every minute we lose discussing this, someone dies.

Alf   Without obeying orders there is no peace, there is chaos, do you get that? Fucking hell, just as well they don't give arms to people like you, you're nothing but an insubordinate –

Unni I'll let you shag me, Alf. Here on the beach, in a motel, in the toilets at work, wherever you want. I'll let you have me. Not now, but I will. I promise. I'll let you have me, just like I let Hagen, if that's what you want. I'll even give you a sneak preview.

She lifts up her top, exposing her breasts.

Alf Cover yourself up, you idiot. Do you want someone to see you?

Unni Get the fuck out of my way. Let's go.

Alf Who do you take me for, Unni? What is this indecency? This is attempted corruption. You've crossed the line, you really have.

*The phone on **Unni**'s belt rings.*

Alf Answer it.

Unni *recomposes herself. She's about to answer the phone but **Alf** grabs it from her and answers it himself.*

Alf Hello? . . . Yes, it's me. Yes, Colonel. Six hundred metres from the shore . . . in Utvika . . . What? Storoya? Certainly, Colonel. We'll be there.

Hangs up.

The Special Forces teams are meeting at Storoya. They'll launch the operation from there.

Unni From Storoya? But it's much further from the island . . .

Alf He said we should stay where we are.

Unni Why don't they use the small boats from here . . .

Alf Where are the car keys?

Unni *throws them on the ground.*

Alf *bends over to pick them up.*

Alf   I'll keep these. Now stay quiet. I don't want to hear another word from you today. Shut up and obey your orders. Understood? You slut.

Unni *stares him down angrily, but says nothing.*

13.

At the farm.

Inga *and* **Petter** *are sitting watching the television footage.*

With beer.

Inga *watches on, astonished at what she's seeing.*

Petter *shouts like a football fan watching a match.*

Petter   He's taken over an entire island? One man? What're they on about? Heavily armed or not, who gives a shit. What are they waiting for? Just take him out. Don't you have a helicopter? A helicopter. Why don't they send one? Where are the police, down the pub playing darts? Get a machine gun, a bazooka, just take the little prick out!

Inga   Can you not talk like that when I'm around? Go to the pub, swear as much as you like, but not here.

Petter   And these fucking journalists keep crying. Why don't you actually show us something, send someone to film the actual – if I was down there, that son of a bitch wouldn't last one –

Inga   If you were *down there*? This isn't a cowboy film.

Petter *watches the news for a few moments and then starts shouting again.*

Petter   I'm gonna go beat up that Moroccan. They're all the same, pieces of shit.

Inga   Don't shout! Now's not the time. You're not at a football match. The window's open.

Petter   So? Who's gonna hear me? We're in the middle of the countryside. There's no one around.

Inga   Apart from the neighbour.

Petter   He's not even here. He left this morning in his van –

He stops.

Thinks.

For a few moments we only hear the sound of the television.

Wait. What did they say earlier?

Inga   That he's taken over the entire island.

Petter   No, earlier. About the explosion in Oslo.

Inga *isn't listening to him.*

She's watching television.

Petter   They said the bomb was in a van.

Inga   Umm, did they?

Petter   A van. Italian brand.

Inga   Yeah, I think so.

Petter   They definitely did.

Inga *keeps watching television.*

Petter   I'm going to have a look.

Inga   What? Where?

Petter   The guy's farm. The troll's.

Inga   What's that got to do with anything?

Petter   He has a van.

Inga   So? Are you insane? They mention a van and you go snooping around our neighbour's things?

Petter   It was Italian-made.

Inga   You've really got straw for brains, don't you, Petter. We are nothing, remember that.

Inga *points to the television.*

This sort of stuff doesn't happen here. Understood?

Petter   I'll just look through the windows. Pop them open a tiny bit.

He picks up a screwdriver.

Inga   Oh sure. Spying on people as usual. You're just a creep. Any chance you get, there you are. When will you learn to mind your own business? Always eavesdropping, listening in . . .

Petter   I just want to see what's in there.

Inga   We should never pry into other people's homes. It's a crime, you know that? What did our parents teach us? Leave other people alone. They are not us. We must respect that. Everyone does what they want, believes what they want. There's space for everyone. We all have our freedom, but everyone needs their own space. Good morning, good night, that's it. That's what they taught us.

Petter   Yes, but . . .

Inga   I don't know him, this guy. I've seen him once, maybe twice. I don't want to know what's in there. I don't care. He could just as well not be there.

Petter   Well, I'm going.

Inga   No you will not. You will not because Dad is here and he is watching you. Mum is here and she's watching you too. You won't go because you are Norwegian. From a Norwegian family. If I see you even as much as walk through that gate, I will call the police. I'll report you. I don't care if you're my brother.

Petter *hesitates for a moment.*

Inga   You should be ashamed of yourself. You voyeur. Do you have a brain up there? They're gunning these kids down like animals. Don't you feel like crying? Sit down here, next to your sister. Look at what's happening. I feel sick. Do you still not get it? I'm tired and I don't feel well. I'm ill. I'm worried that I'm seriously ill. Just stay with me, for once.

Petter *looks at her. Hesitates.*

He puts the screwdriver back down.

He sits down.

14.

Gunnar *and* **Malin**'s *home.*

The television is still on.

The tension is unbearable.

Malin   They must've killed her.

Gunnar   Please Malin, just . . . please.

Malin   I can feel it. They've killed her.

Gunnar   There is no reason, absolutely no plausible reason, to think so.

Malin   There's a mother's intuition.

Malin *looks at her husband with hatred.*

Silence.

Gunnar   Why are you looking at me like that?

Malin   She didn't want to go.

Gunnar   Don't start this again.

Malin   She said she thought it was lame. And you made her go.

Gunnar   So it's my fault now? Have I carried out the terrorist attack?

Malin   Why did you send her, Gunnar? Why did you insist?

Gunnar   Stop it. What's the point?

Malin   Why did you insist?

Gunnar   She was all over the place . . . you said so too. Always with those friends of hers, those idiots with tonnes of money who go shopping with their families in New York on weekends. She was obsessed with fashion, with designer clothing. With her iPhone. She wanted a Rolex. Remember? The cringiest status symbol imaginable. And she'd treat us like we were bloody peasants. She despised me, she despised you. Our way of life. She despised everything about us. How we ate, what we bought. She lost touch with reality.

Malin   And you sent her to be slaughtered because you hate iPhones?

Gunnar   Don't even joke about that, Malin. Don't you dare joke about it.

Malin   Because of the Rolex?

Gunnar   I'm suffering over here too. I'm also worried for Kristine.

Malin   You never cared about Kristine! Every time she interrupted your work you'd complain. Whenever it was your turn to take her to school, you'd miraculously disappear. You've never taken her to a party. Or a birthday. You talk about her friends, but have you actually ever met them? You talk about her friends because *I've* told you about them. You don't know your own daughter. Your daughter is mine. You've never been involved, not even once. Actually yes, once, fifteen days ago, to blackmail her and force her to go to a fucking socialist camp.

Gunnar *looks at her in silence.*

Malin   Could you not have just continued not giving a shit? Just carried on shagging sixth form students? Yes, don't deny it, I know how it is, you don't do it earlier because they're underage, and as timid as you are, you wouldn't dare. But in sixth form, ah, those extra uni prep classes in autumn . . . but I don't give a fuck, Gunnar. I have never given a fuck. I only care about Kristine.

Gunnar   She'll be fine. I can feel it.

Malin   You have never felt a thing in your life. You've never felt love, you've never felt anything – and you're gonna feel something now? You are a cold, self-centred man who makes shit jokes, and spends all his time reading useless books, all so he can tell others that they're ignorant. Just like you tell your students, me, Kristine, everyone.

Gunnar *is still silent.*

Malin   Tell me why you sent her, Gunnar! I need to know.

Gunnar   I wanted her to come back with some sort of . . . faith.

Malin   Faith? What faith?

Gunnar *does not respond.*

Malin   I want to know what faith you wanted to indoctrinate her into, Gunnar. And do not say socialism or I'll spit in your face.

Gunnar   Spit in my face then.

Malin   That's not a faith. That is politics.

Gunnar   For people like you who don't believe in it, maybe.

Malin   Why, do you believe in it?

Gunnar   Yes, Malin, I believe in it. I believe that life should be spent in the pursuit of something greater. It's not just about us, we're all in it together. We can't just think about ourselves. We need a meaning, a sense of direction. Otherwise we're lost, and things get hard, what do we do? What do we cling to?

Malin   *This* is things getting hard. What are you clinging to? Socialism?

Gunnar   Partly. That too. I hope our daughter is safe. That she is safe, right now. And that after this disaster, maybe even thanks to this disaster, she becomes a better person. I have faith, I do. I'm not embarrassed to say so.

Malin   Fuck you, Gunnar. Fuck you. Muslims killing our children? They have faith. They have faith in their fucking God. They plant bombs in the name of God. They rape women. They pour petrol on people. And you know why they do it? Because they have faith. Just like you. Men of faith. The Nazis had faith. Fuck faith. The communists had faith. Look what happened. Faith is the worst sickness a person can have. It is a parasite to the human mind. Faith makes me sick. Because humans are nothing, and we should believe in nothing: no God, no Allah, no socialism, no fascism. Nothing. We should just know that we'll die. That's the truth, everything else is just a heap of shit, made up by stupid and presumptuous people like you.

Malin *is exhausted after shouting.*

She collapses onto the sofa.

Gunnar   Why are you attacking me, Malin? Why are you taking it out on me?

Malin   You sent your daughter to die. Why? For a cause that even you, deep down, know is a lie.

Gunnar   No, it's not a lie, Malin. It's not.

Malin   All beliefs are a lie. If we got rid of them, all of them, maybe we would all get along a bit better.

Gunnar   We would spend our time killing each other like dogs.

Malin   Well, what are we doing now? Look. Look at the television. What's that? What are we doing?

Gunnar   I *hope*, Malin. I hope that . . .

Malin   Where do you think your hope will get you? In the ground, Gunnar. We all end up there. You fucking idiot, what were you thinking? You never gave a fuck about her, and then when you finally do something . . .

Sobbing, **Malin** *gets up and lunges at him, striking him.* **Gunnar** *tries to defend himself.*

Gunnar   Calm down, Malin. Calm down.

The phone rings.

Both of them stop and stare at it.

Gunnar *picks up.*

Gunnar   Hello . . . yes, yes it's us. So? No, her mobile is off . . . the name is the one I gave you earlier . . . what do you mean you can't find it? Check again . . . it has to be there . . . it has to. It's there . . . yes, yes, I'll stay calm . . . OK . . . you'll let us know . . . what the situation is. Are you sending officers in? What? Why can't you tell me anything? We're her parents, we have to know . . . listen to me . . . OK, OK. But please call us. We really can't bear this. Please don't leave us out of the loop.

Malin   What did they say?

Gunnar   They can't find Kristine in the camp register.

Malin   Idiots . . . they're fucking incompetent . . .

Gunnar   The Special Forces have just landed on the island. They said it should be over soon.

Malin   Soon? When, Gunnar?

Gunnar *leaves, shaking his head.*

Malin *collapses onto the sofa again.*

The television continues blaring.

15.

The farm.

Inga *and* **Petter** *are face to face.*

Petter   They said he's Scandinavian.

Inga   They said he's Muslim.

Petter   They were wrong. He's Scandinavian. Thirty years old. Blond.

Inga   Maybe they're wrong again.

Petter   Well, they would know, wouldn't they?

Inga   Did they get him?

Petter   They did.

Inga   Did they show it on TV?

Petter *shakes his head.*

Petter   Sixty-nine children killed. He did target practice for over an hour. Some were shot as they ran away. And if they weren't dead, he finished them off by shooting them in the head.

Inga *lets out a sudden scream.*

Inga   I've got goosebumps. One of us. It's horrendous. I would've preferred it to be a Muslim. Are you sure? One of us?

Petter *stares at her.*

Inga   Why are you looking at me like that?

Petter   You know why.

Inga   No I don't.

Silence.

Inga   Don't get any ideas. It's not true. It's all in your head, in your weird brain. Poor Petter.

Petter   I swear, if it's him, you're getting it.

Inga   I'm your older sister. How dare you, Petter? Don't you dare talk to me like that.

Petter   I'll lose it.

Inga   Shame on you. I'm ashamed of you. I wish Dad could hear you now.

Petter   I don't care about Dad. I'll do it.

Inga   Try . . .

Petter   I will. I'll make you bleed. I'll beat you to a pulp.

Inga   You poor, perverted idiot.

Inga *turns on her heels and exits.*

Petter *is furious.*

Petter   You better pray it's not him.

16.

Malin *is crying.*

Gunnar *enters.*

Malin   So?

Gunnar   They still haven't identified them all. They still can't find her.

Malin   Who was the attacker?

Gunnar   Apparently he was white. Nordic. Possibly one of us.

Silence.

Malin   Why?

Gunnar *shrugs.*

Gunnar   They hit the youth branch of the only European socialist party that isn't full of wankers. It must've been a right-wing plot. My dad would've been sure of it. The old communist.

Malin   So will Kristine become a socialist martyr then, Gunnar?

Gunnar   Oh please just shut up, would you? They don't know anything. They haven't found her. How can you say something like that? They said they don't know anything yet.

Malin   My baby, my Kristine. She's been killed.

Gunnar   Shut up!

Malin   A Norwegian has shot her in the head. And another Norwegian sent her there to be shot at.

Gunnar *explodes.*

Gunnar   Enough! I've been putting up with this for hours, now stop! Please. This is the last afternoon we'll spend together, you can be sure of that. No more afternoons, evenings, or nights. We've ruined it. I never want to see you again. I'll get rid of all your photographs, because whatever there was between us is gone. This day is all that's left, that's all you are to me, what's happened today. Nothing and no one will be able to erase it from my memory, from my mind, from my life until I die . . . which I hope happens very, very soon . . .

The phone rings.

They both freeze and stare at it.

Gunnar *moves to pick it up.*

Malin *indicates for him not to do so.*

He stops.

She picks up.

Malin   Hello? . . . *Kristine?* . . .

Gunnar *looks at her.*

Malin She's alive . . . yes, my baby, yes . . . don't cry . . .
don't cry . . . It doesn't matter . . . nothing else matters, the
important thing is you're alive . . . no, your father and I
aren't angry . . . the important thing is you're still here.
Worried? We've been through hell, Kristine, hell . . . your
father and I, both of us . . . were you frightened? What
happened? Why did you not pick up? Why didn't you call
right away? Why didn't you . . . what? Oh. Oh . . . I see . . . I
see . . . no, no that doesn't matter . . . of course you could've
never . . . you've couldn't have known . . . of course. Come
home now, though, Kristine . . . no, we're not angry . . . but
please get on the first train, for the love of God, come home
. . . Mummy needs to give you a hug . . . right away. Right
away. As quick as you can, my sweetheart . . . we'll be waiting
here . . . yes, Daddy too . . . we'll be there.

Malin *hangs up.*

She bursts into tears.

Gunnar Is she OK? Is she hurt?

Malin She's OK.

Gunnar Oh thank God. Thank God. Not even a scratch?

Malin *shakes her head.*

Gunnar *slowly breathes out a sigh of relief.*

Malin She wasn't there.

Gunnar She wasn't there?

Malin No.

Gunnar On the island?

Malin No. She never went.

Gunnar Well, where was she?

Malin She lied to us.

Gunnar   Where did she go? I took her to the station.

Malin   She changed trains at Oslo. She was in a tattoo parlour in Lillestrom.

Gunnar   Lillestrom?

Malin   She got a tattoo of a Rolex on her back.

Gunnar   Oh sweet Jesus. What colour?

Malin   She didn't say.

Gunnar   It doesn't matter. It doesn't matter.

Malin   She disobeyed you. Good girl. Good girl.

Gunnar   A Rolex. Wonderful. A Rolex on her back.

Gunnar *is now crying too.*

Gunnar   I'll buy her a real one. She deserves it. I'll get her a gold one.

A Month Later

17.

Honefoss Police Station.

Alf *is at the desk.*

He is reading the sports section.

Unni *appears.*

She is in civilian clothes.

Alf *looks up.*

He checks his watch.

Alf   You're half an hour late.

Unni *doesn't respond.*

Alf   After four weeks' holiday.

Unni   I didn't ask for it.

Alf   We gave it to you so you wouldn't have any more hysterical breakdowns.

Unni   I didn't ask for holiday.

Alf   And now no uniform . . . half an hour late and no uniform.

Unni *clocks the newspaper.*

Unni   You don't seem like you were that concerned.

Alf *closes the newspaper.*

Alf   I could've got rid of you for how you behaved, Unni. I didn't even file a report. I've drawn a veil over that whole day. But things are going to change from now on. I will no longer tolerate that sort of behaviour.

Alf *looks at her.*

Unni *is looking away.*

Alf *changes approach.*

Alf   Did you go to Greece with your family? Did you have a good holiday?

Unni   I haven't.

Alf   Had a good holiday?

Unni   Drawn a veil. I think about it all the time.

Alf   What are you talking about?

Unni   We were there, Alf. We were six hundred metres from the island . . .

Alf   Listen, I have absolutely no intention of getting back into this. I know what you're going to say.

Unni   We could hear their cries and the gunshots and you refused to take any initiative.

Alf *raises his voice.*

Alf   It wasn't fucking me! It was the guys in Oslo! The order was to leave it to the Special Forces.

Unni   Who someone decided should set off from much further away. And then the engine on their boat fucking broke.

Alf   And what the fuck have I got to do with that? I wasn't the maintenance guy.

Unni   They had to do three transfers, *three*, before anyone could get to the island. Over half an hour later.

Alf   It was unlucky.

Unni   He was killing a child a minute. How many could we have saved if you had just listened to me?

Alf   None, judging by how you use firearms. They would've awarded you a nice posthumous medal.

Unni   He surrendered as soon as he saw the police! No resistance.

Alf   We couldn't have known that.

Unni   Our children could have been there.

Alf   Are yours socialists?

Unni   What's that got to do with it?

Alf   So they couldn't have been there then.

Unni   What does that mean?

Alf   That's the risk you run. Getting political.

Unni   What are you talking about?

Alf   What I just said. Want to go into politics? You've got to accept that people might come after you. Try and shoot you.

Unni   You hate socialists, don't you?

Alf   I am apolitical. I don't give a fuck about politics or trade unions. They can all kill each other for all I care.

Unni   Do you know what this guy wrote? That sixty per cent of police sympathise with his ideas . . .

Alf   Not in my case.

Unni   That when he carried out the attack, the police would turn a blind eye. Isn't that exactly what happened?

Alf   No. There were precise orders. Now go and get into uniform or I'll report you for failing to return to your post.

Unni *is furious.*

She throws a piece of paper down onto the desk.

Alf *looks at it.*

Alf   What is this?

Unni   My resignation.

Alf *looks at her in silence.*

A moment of tension.

Alf   OK. I will pass this on to Central Command in Oslo. I'll let you know if they accept it. Go and get into uniform.

Unni   No chance, Alf. I'm leaving.

Alf   That's desertion.

Unni   Call it whatever the fuck you want. I refuse to obey your orders any longer.

Unni *turns on her heels and exits.*

Alf *remains seated, staring at her.*

He shakes his head.

Spits on the ground.

Continues reading the newspaper.

18.

The farm.

Inga *is in bed.*

She is emaciated and sick.

One of her eyes is bandaged.

Petter *enters.*

Inga   Can you pass me my fleece?

Petter *hands it to her.*

Inga   It's not that warm anymore, is it?

Petter   No.

Inga   Summer's over.

Petter Tomorrow's St Bartholomew's Day. Twenty-third of August. Ram slaughter.

Inga Yeah . . .

Silence.

What did the doctor say before he left?

Petter He was positive. Said you're doing well.

Inga You're a terrible liar, Petter. You just can't tell lies can you?

Petter I really can't.

Inga Do you think I don't know? I know how I feel.

Petter It's gonna be alright. You'll get better, you'll see.

Inga Sure, sure. You can go now. I'll manage.

Petter *sits next to her.*

Petter I'm staying here.

Inga No, go to the pub. It's still early.

Petter I don't want to see anyone. I don't feel like going out. I haven't felt like it since that day.

Inga Good. You went out too much before.

Petter Something broke that day, and it can't be fixed. Did you see what he wrote on the internet? Twelve thousand pages. Why had no one found them? He wanted to kill all the Muslims.

Inga That's our fault, too. Our own prejudice.

Petter You're not prejudiced.

Inga Oh, yes I am. Deep down, I am too. Otherwise I would've married the Moroccan. I actually quite liked him.

Petter Really?

Inga Yes.

Petter   He wanted to kill them all.

Inga   And he started with those who protected them.

Petter   He was a troll.

Inga   But we didn't know that.

Petter   He was using the fertiliser to make bombs.

Inga   We couldn't know that. We were too far away.

Petter   Sometimes I'd watch him with those binoculars.

Inga   I've thrown those away.

Petter   He was here, right under our noses, and none of us stopped him.

Inga   Well, we don't even know his name . . .

Petter   Well, now we do, his name was –

Inga   Don't say it. That name doesn't deserve to be uttered by anyone. Ever again.

Petter   I could've gone to check. Not just that day. Before that, too. Maybe I could've . . .

Petter *hangs his head.*

Inga   I'm glad you didn't. Some things just shouldn't be done, simple as. That's what our parents taught us. And our grandparents taught them. And our great grandparents taught them. Good morning, good night. Respect.

Petter   But if I could go back, I'd stop him. Fuck our grandparents and our great grandparents. I'd go and find him. I'd kill him. I cried for those kids. As if they were my brothers and sisters. I've never felt like that before.

Inga   No, you're wrong. Respect. At all costs. That's our country. That's how we are.

Petter   I think you talk about respect, but you don't give a shit about anyone else.

Inga   Maybe not, Petter. But that's respect too. And we should all push on as before. Even after what has happened.

Pause.

Inga   Plus, I give a shit about you. About my family.

Petter   I'm so sorry for what I did to you. I lost my mind.

Inga   My eye is the only thing that'll get better.

Petter   I didn't know you were sick. I swear. Otherwise . . .

Inga   Let's not think about it. Promise me one thing.

Petter   What?

Inga   That you'll get married, Petter. I can't stand the thought of you all alone.

Petter   Well, I'll have you.

Inga   I won't be around much longer.

Petter   No, Inga . . .

Inga   You'll manage. You've grown up now. A little late, but you've become a man.

19.

Gunnar *and* **Malin**'s *house.*

A box on the floor.

Gunnar *is on the phone.*

Gunnar   It wasn't just me. We decided together, Kristine. Yes, but she's also right, I'm a difficult man. Always working . . . well, I put barriers up between me and others . . . no, I'm serious . . . I also slept with some students, OK? What can I say, clearly that's the type of person I've become. But that has nothing to do with socialism. For me, those murdered kids are heroes. They believed in equality, in loyalty. As for their idea . . . no, don't just identify socialism

with me. There's the bigger picture, and I'm just one person
. . . I've not been a good father, I know. But believe me,
Kristine, that day, I would've given my life to make sure you
were safe. I hate that Rolex. But it saved you, and I'll buy
you a real one, OK? Look, I've got to go, your mother's
arriving.

He hangs up.

Malin *enters.*

Malin   I was hoping you'd have already left.

Gunnar   It's all packed in the van. I'm leaving.

Malin *spots the box.*

Malin   Take that one too.

Gunnar   That's a gift for you.

Malin   Give it to one of your female students.

Gunnar   Please, just open it.

Malin   Whatever it is, I'm not changing my mind. It's over.

Gunnar   Nor am I. It's not about that, Malin. Just open
the box.

Malin *opens the box. There is a kitten inside.*

Gunnar   I hope it keeps you company. And that it's nicer
and more faithful than me.

We hear it miaowing.

Let it play. It needs to exercise.

Malin *picks up the kitten.*

Gunnar   I bought it on Strandgaten.

Malin *gives a small nod.*

Gunnar   It's a Norwegian Forest Cat.

Gunnar *leaves.*

Malin *watches him go.*

The door shuts.

Lights out.